A Bear Called Trouble

Written by Jenny Feely

Illustrated by Meredith Thomas

Flying Start
to Literacy®

Contents

Chapter 1
An invitation arrives

"Whoopee!" yelled Dad. "We've been invited to Grandpa's birthday – and it's a fancy dress party. I love fancy dress parties."

"That's wonderful," said Mum.
"I'll go as a mermaid. What will
you all go as?"

"I'll go as a seal," said Hannah.

"I will dress as a polar explorer,"
said David. "What will you dress
up as, Dad?"

"It's a secret," said Dad.
"You will have to wait and see!"

"Can you give us a clue?"
asked David.

"I'll need a warm costume,"
said Dad. "It's cold all the time
where Grandpa lives, even in
summer."

"That's because Grandpa lives near the North Pole," said Mum.

"I can't wait to visit Grandpa," said Hannah.

"And I can't wait to go in the plane to get there," said David.

Chapter 2
All dressed up

When they arrived, everyone
unpacked their costumes.

"I'm a seal," said Hannah, as she
slapped her flippers together.
"Erff, erff."

Just then Dad sprang into
the room.

"I'm a fierce polar bear. Rraaa!"
he growled. "I can smell a seal.
Polar bears eat seals."

"Help!" yelled Hannah.

"Rraaa!" growled Dad, as he
tried to sit on David. "Polar bears
are not afraid of explorers either."

Dad chased everyone around.

After a while, Dad stopped chasing everyone and took off his polar bear head.

"It sure is hot in there," said Dad, wiping his face. "Phew!"

"Perhaps you need a different costume," said Mum.

"But this costume is perfect," said Dad. "Grandpa will be surprised when he sees a cute polar bear at his party."

"Polar bears may look cute, but they are wild animals," said Mum. "They are very dangerous."

"Well I'm not dangerous," said Dad. "I'm the world's friendliest polar bear."

"But you look like a real polar bear," said Mum. "Rangers go all around town looking for polar bears. If they see a bear, the rangers make loud noises to scare it away."

"I will tell the rangers I'm not a real polar bear," said Dad.

"But if a real bear is not scared away, they shoot it with a tranquilliser dart to put it to sleep. Then they take it out of town. I think you're just asking for trouble," said Mum.

"Trouble," said Dad. "That's who I'll be – Trouble, the polar bear."

Chapter 3
Trouble in the street

When it was time to leave for the party, everyone decided to walk as it was a fine night and it was still light outside.

"Hey, this polar bear costume is really warm," said Dad.

"My costume is warm too,"
said Hannah.

"And these polar bear feet don't
slip on the ice," said Dad.
"I like being a polar bear."

Dad got down on the ground and
began to growl like a real bear.
He chased Hannah and David.

"Look out!" David yelled. "Here
comes Trouble."

Just then there was a very loud noise.
Everyone jumped and looked around.

"What was that?" said Mum.

"Don't worry," said Dad.
"I'm sure it was nothing."

But Mum was worried.

Chapter 4
More trouble for Dad

There was another loud noise
and two rangers drove up.

"Beep! Beep!" The rangers tooted
their car horn loudly.
"Get out of the way, the bear's
going to attack," they said.
"Stay very still while we shoot
a tranquilliser dart into him."

"Stop!" yelled Mum, but it was
too late.

There was a whooshing noise as
the ranger shot a tranquilliser dart
at Dad.

"You missed," yelled one of
the rangers.

"No, I didn't," shouted the other
ranger. "I hit him in the foot, but
the tranquilliser dart has fallen out."

"That won't knock a polar
bear out," said the first ranger.

But Dad dropped like a rock. The
rangers jumped out and grabbed
a net from the back of the truck.

"Stay back," they yelled, as they
slid a net under Dad. "We will
call a helicopter to take this bear
out of town."

"Stop! Stop!" yelled Mum.
"That's not a polar bear.
That's my husband!"

"What?" said the rangers.

They looked at us. We all nodded.

"We are on our way to a fancy dress party," said Hannah.

Very carefully, the rangers took the net off Dad. They turned him over and took off his polar bear head.

Dad was snoring happily.

"It's the tranquilliser," said the rangers. "Luckily he didn't get a very big dose. But he will sleep for hours. You will need help to get him to the party."

The rangers loaded Dad into their truck and drove us to the party.

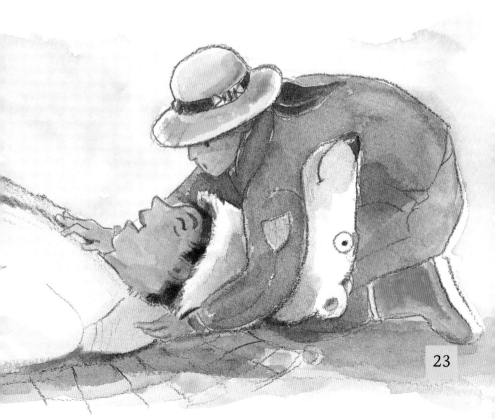

Chapter 5
The perfect costume

At Grandpa's party, everyone said that Dad looked like a real polar bear.

But Dad didn't hear any of them. He was fast asleep.